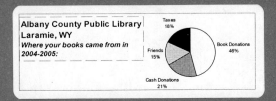

# Islamic
## ART & CULTURE

## Nicola Barber

Chicago, Illinois

09 08 07 06 05
10 9 8 7 6 5 4 3 2 1

Produced for Raintree by White-Thomson Publishing Ltd.
Editorial: Kay Barnham, Nicole Irving, and Louise Galpine
Design: Simon Borrough and Ron Kamen
Illustrations: Tinstar Design
Picture Research: Elaine Fuoco-Lang
Originated by Ambassador Litho Ltd.
Printed and bound in Hong Kong, China by South China Printing Company

**Library of Congress Cataloging-in-Publication Data**
Barber, Nicola.
  Islamic art and culture / Nicola Barber.
    p. cm. -- (World art and culture)
  Includes bibliographical references and index.
  ISBN 1-4109-1105-5
  1.  Art, Islamic. 2.  Architecture, Islamic. 3.  Islamic
Empire--History.  I. Title. II. Series: World art & culture.
  N6260.B3674 2005
  709'.17'67--dc22

                                  2004008073

**Acknowledgements**
The publishers would like to thank the following for permission to reproduce photographs: Art Archive pp. 19 (British Library), 30 (Museum of Islamic Art Cairo / Dagli Orti), 16 (National Museum Damascus Syria / Dagli Orti), 12 (Private Collection / Eileen Tweed), 31, 42, 48 (Victoria and Albert Museum London / Sally Chappell); Bridgeman Art Library pp. 21 (Dost Yayinlari), 17 (Bibliothèque Nationale, Paris, France), 18 (Detroit Institute of Arts, USA, Gift of Robert H. Tannahill in memory of Dr. W.R. Valentiner), 33, 37; Corbis pp. 28 (Angelo Hornak), 14 (Archivo Iconografico, S.A.), 43 (Arthur Thévenart), 22 (Carmen Redondo/CORBIS), 50 (Charles & Josette Lenars), 23, 47 (Chris Hellier), 44 (Chris Lisle), 13 (David H. Wells), 11 (Gérard Degeorge), 39 (John and Lisa Merrill), 15 (Lindsay Hebberd), 40 (Nevada Wier), 24 (Nik Wheeler), 25 (Origlia Franco / Corbis Sygma), 37 (Owen Franken), 27 (Roger Wood), 45 (Ruggero Vanni), 9 (Werner Forman), 26 (Yann Arthus-Bertrand); Harcourt p. 7; Popperfoto.com p. 5; Topfoto p. 51; Werner Forman Archive pp. 35 (Museum of Islamic Art, Cairo), 1, 8, 10, 20, 29, 34, 41.

Cover photograph of a tile with hares reproduced with kind permission of Scala Archives, and of background tiles, reproduced with kind permission of Werner Forman.

The publisher would like to thank Dr. Tim Insoll for his assistance in the preparation of this book.

Every effort has been made to contact copyright holders of any material reproduced in this book. Any omissions will be rectified in subsequent printings if notice is given to the publisher.

Some words appear in bold, **like this.** You can find out what they mean by looking in the glossary.

# Contents

# Introduction

The Islamic faith began almost 1,400 years ago in Arabia, when the Prophet Muhammad is said to have received messages from God (Allah). Muhammad began to preach the central message of Islam: there is no other God but God, and Muhammad is the messenger of God. The meaning of the Arabic word *Islam* is "submission," and those who converted to Islam agreed to submit to the will of God. They became known as Muslims. Islam quickly spread from the Arabian peninsula, extending its influence to Spain in the west and, eventually, to Southeast Asia in the east.

## Islamic art

The term *Islamic art* covers a broad range of traditions, from metalwork to carpet weaving, from **calligraphy** to architecture. It includes religious art, as well as art made by and for Muslims, objects made by Muslims for **patrons** of other faiths, and objects made for Muslim patrons by workers of other faiths. Islamic art is found across a wide range of cultures, from Spain and northern Africa to Central Asia and Anatolia (Turkey) to Southeast Asia. The Islamic religion provides a common link between these cultures.

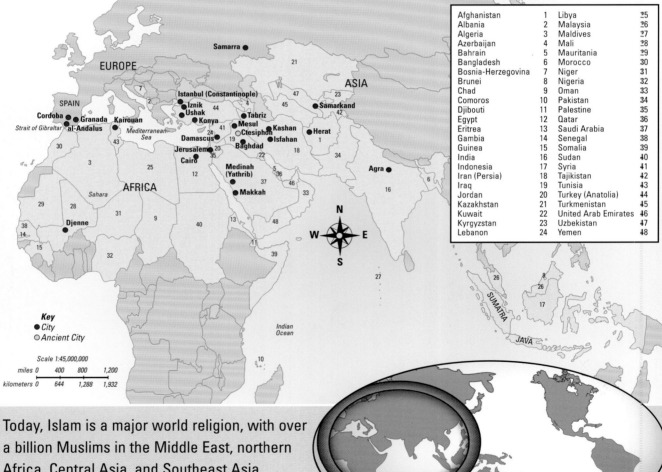

| | | | |
|---|---|---|---|
| Afghanistan | 1 | Libya | 25 |
| Albania | 2 | Malaysia | 26 |
| Algeria | 3 | Maldives | 27 |
| Azerbaijan | 4 | Mali | 28 |
| Bahrain | 5 | Mauritania | 29 |
| Bangladesh | 6 | Morocco | 30 |
| Bosnia-Herzegovina | 7 | Niger | 31 |
| Brunei | 8 | Nigeria | 32 |
| Chad | 9 | Oman | 33 |
| Comoros | 10 | Pakistan | 34 |
| Djibouti | 11 | Palestine | 35 |
| Egypt | 12 | Qatar | 36 |
| Eritrea | 13 | Saudi Arabia | 37 |
| Gambia | 14 | Senegal | 38 |
| Guinea | 15 | Somalia | 39 |
| India | 16 | Sudan | 40 |
| Indonesia | 17 | Syria | 41 |
| Iran (Persia) | 18 | Tajikistan | 42 |
| Iraq | 19 | Tunisia | 43 |
| Jordan | 20 | Turkey (Anatolia) | 44 |
| Kazakhstan | 21 | Turkmenistan | 45 |
| Kuwait | 22 | United Arab Emirates | 46 |
| Kyrgyzstan | 23 | Uzbekistan | 47 |
| Lebanon | 24 | Yemen | 48 |

**Key**
- City
- Ancient City

Scale 1:45,000,000

| miles 0 | 400 | 800 | 1,200 |
|---|---|---|---|
| kilometers 0 | 644 | 1,288 | 1,932 |

Today, Islam is a major world religion, with over a billion Muslims in the Middle East, northern Africa, Central Asia, and Southeast Asia. Countries in which Islam is a major religion today are shown in pink on the map above. Millions more Muslims live in non-Islamic countries across the world.

Muslims crowd around the **Ka'bah** shrine in the Grand **Mosque** at Makkah. Arabs believed that this shrine had been set up by Ibrahim (Abraham) and was full of idols of gods and goddesses. According to tradition, when Muhammad destroyed the idols, the shrine became one of the holiest places of Islam.

## Arabia

The traditional heartland of Islam is centered around Arabia and the Middle East. Islam began in the 7th century C.E. in the Arabian town of Makkah (in present-day Saudi Arabia; also known as Mecca). As now, much of Arabia was harsh, **arid** desert. In the southwest was a mountainous area, now part of Yemen, where there was enough rainfall for farming. The Romans called this area *Arabia Felix* ("fruitful Arabia") because of its reputation as a land of great wealth and prosperity.

When the Prophet Muhammad was born, the majority of the inhabitants of Arabia, known as Arabs, lived in settlements built near a water source such as an **oasis**. However, large numbers of Arabs, called Bedouin, lived **nomadic** or seminomadic lives. They moved from place to place with their flocks of camels, sheep, and goats, looking for grazing areas. Most Arabs worshiped many different gods and goddesses.

## Beyond Arabia

The northern edge of the Arabian peninsula was bordered by two great empires. To the west lay the **Byzantine Empire,** with its capital city of Constantinople, now Istanbul. To the east was the **Sassanian Empire,** which covered Persia (modern-day Iran). Its capital city was Ctesiphon.

The Byzantines and Sassanians were frequently at war with each other, but the Muslim Arabs achieved victory over both their powerful neighbors. As Islam began to spread and establish itself, the first Islamic works of art were produced.

## The Prophet Muhammad

Muhammad was born about 570 C.E. in Makkah. He became a merchant and led an ordinary life until the age of 40. It was then that he is said to have received the first of the messages from God, brought to him by the Angel Jibril (Gabriel). When Muhammad began to preach the messages of God, some people converted to Islam, but others treated Muslims with great suspicion and hostility. In 622 the Prophet Muhammad and his followers decided to leave Makkah. They went to Yathrib, a city about 250 miles (400 kilometers) to the north. This was to be Muhammad's home for the rest of his life, and it was renamed Madinah, meaning "City of the Prophet." Muhammad died in 632.

## The succession

After Muhammad's death, there was disagreement about who should succeed him. Muhammad's father-in-law and closest friend, Abu Bakr, was chosen as the first *Khalifah* ("successor"). He died two years later, and three more *Khalifahs* followed before the Umayyad family seized power in 661. The Umayyads founded the first Islamic dynasty (meaning that the title of *Khalifah* was passed from father to son).

## The spread of Islam

In the years following the death of the Prophet Muhammad, Islam spread rapidly. The Arabian peninsula was quickly conquered, and Muslim rule extended across Palestine and Syria (formerly controlled by the **Byzantines**) and Iraq and Iran (formerly controlled by the **Sassanians**). The Muslim armies took control of another Byzantine province, Egypt, in 641, and extended their power along the Mediterranean coast. The inhabitants of this area of northern Africa were called Berbers, and many converted to Islam. By 750, Muslim lands extended from northwestern Africa and Spain in the west to Afghanistan in the east.

### ◈ Shia and Sunni

The disagreement over Muhammad's successor caused a division in the Islamic world that continues to this day. Most Muslims believed that the *Khalifah* should be the person best able to uphold the customs and traditions (the sunna) of Islam. These Muslims became known as **Sunni.** Others, known as **Shia,** believed that only someone from the same family as Muhammad should succeed the Prophet.

Circa 570: Birth of the Prophet Muhammad.

622: *Hijrah* ("migration") from Makkah to Madinah.

632: Death of the Prophet Muhammad.

661–750, Umayyad dynasty: The Dome of the Rock and the Great **Mosque** in Damascus are built.

711: Muslim invasion of Spain.

The Dome of the Rock in Jerusalem was built in the 7th century. The holiest shrine in the Islamic world, this monument is an octagonal (eight-sided) building topped with a dome covered with gold. Its walls are decorated with marble and **mosaics.**

## The Umayyads

The Umayyads established their capital at Damascus in Syria, and it was under their rule that the first major Islamic monuments were built, including the Dome of the Rock in Jerusalem. They were removed from power by the Abbasids in 750.

During the 8th and 9th centuries, the Abbasids built a new capital at Baghdad in Iraq, which became a center of the arts and learning. They held the title of *Khalifah* until the Mongol invasions of 1258.

750–1258, Abbasid dynasty: New capital is founded at Baghdad, which becomes a center of learning and the arts.

756: Abd al-Rahman takes control of al-Andalus. Construction of Great Mosque at Cordoba, in Spain, begins.

Circa 960: Seljuks convert to Islam.

969: Fatimids conquer Egypt. Period of great **opulence** in the arts begins.

## Islam in Spain

In 711, Islamic troops—mostly Berbers from northern Africa—crossed the Strait of Gibraltar and began the Muslim invasion of Spain. They soon established the Muslim province of al-Andalus. In 756 an Umayyad prince named Abd al-Rahman took control of al-Andalus. Abd al-Rahman had made a dramatic escape from Syria after the overthrow of his dynasty by the Abbasids and the murder of the whole Umayyad family. He made his capital at Cordoba, which became a center of the arts and learning during the 9th century.

## The Fatimids and the Seljuks

The power of the Abbasid **Khalifah** was attacked by peoples such as the Seljuks and the Fatimids.

This is the beautiful interior of the Great **Mosque** at Cordoba. Work on the mosque began in the 8th century. The roof of the great prayer hall is supported by double arches, shown here, built from contrasting brick and stone. In the early 16th century, a European-style Gothic chapel was built in the middle of the original mosque.

The Seljuks were Turkish **nomads** from Central Asia who converted to Islam about 960 and went on to create an empire that extended from Anatolia across the Middle East. Under Seljuk rule, art and architecture flourished, particularly pottery at centers such as Kashan in Persia.

The Fatimids came from Tunisia in northern Africa. They took Egypt from the Abbasids in 969 and established their capital at Cairo. The Fatimid court was very wealthy and, under Fatimid rule, Cairo became a very important cultural center.

**1055:** Seljuks enter Baghdad. Under their rule, art and architecture flourish, particularly pottery.

**1206:** Mongol tribes unite under leader Genghis Khan.

**1221:** Genghis Khan invades Samarkand.

**1227:** Death of Genghis Khan.

**1250–1517:** Mamluks (see page 17) rule Egypt. Beautiful **Qur'ans** commissioned for mosques and *madrasahs,* and glass making skills are developed.

## The Mongols and Timurids

The year 1258 is a significant date in the Islamic world. This was when the Mongols invaded Baghdad, finally ending the Abbasid dynasty. The Mongols were tribes of nomads from the grasslands of Central Asia who united under their leader, Genghis Khan, in 1206. Genghis Khan conquered parts of China before starting his attacks on the Islamic lands, destroying towns and cities as he went. His sons continued this work after the death of Genghis in 1227. The Mongols were not Muslims, but many converted to Islam during the 13th century. At its height, the Mongol Empire stretched across the Islamic lands, and many Muslim artists and craftworkers were influenced by new ideas from East Asia.

Mongol power was quite short-lived, but at the end of the 14th century another Mongol leader, Timur the Lame (Tamerlane), tried to reestablish the Mongol Empire. Timur spent much of his life taking part in military campaigns, but he also built many fine buildings at his capital in Samarkand, bringing artists and craftworkers from all over his empire to enrich the city.

## The Safavids

The Safavids established their empire in 1501, when Ismail I captured Tabriz and made it the Safavid capital. The greatest of all the Safavid rulers was **Shah** Abbas I, known as Abbas the Great. He moved the Safavid capital to Isfahan (now in Iran) and built an impressive new city there. Abbas encouraged crafts such as carpet weaving and set up royal workshops where carpets were made for export. After his death, the empire began to decline, and in the 18th century different groups competed for power in the region.

This bowl, decorated with a horse, dates from Fatimid times in Egypt.

1258: Mongols invade Baghdad. Center of book production moves to Iran (Persia).

1369–1405: Timur revives Mongol power. Many mosques built in Samarkand.

1453: Ottomans capture Constantinople and rename it Istanbul. Royal **patronage** ensures production of fine, luxurious goods.

1501: Safavids found their empire, with the capital at Tabriz.

1514: Ottomans defeat Safavids. Many Iranian artists taken to work in royal studios in Istanbul.

## The Ottomans

The Safavids were **Shia Muslims** and were constantly at war with the Ottomans, their **Sunni** neighbors to the west. The Ottomans had been establishing themselves in Anatolia since the 14th century, but their breakthrough came in 1453, when they captured the city of Constantinople from the **Byzantines.** The Ottomans made the city their capital and renamed it Istanbul. The Ottoman court and government were based at the Topkapi Palace in Istanbul, which also became a center for the arts, with court studios and workshops producing luxury goods such as jewelry, metalwork, and fine **textiles.**

The Ottoman Empire was under attack throughout the 18th and 19th centuries, finally collapsing in 1918, when its provinces were occupied by European powers at the end of World War I.

## The Mughals

In India, a Muslim empire was founded in 1526 by Babur, who claimed to be directly descended from both Genghis Khan and Timur. At its height, the Mughal Empire covered the whole of India except for the southern tip.

The six great Mughal emperors—Babur, Humayan, Akbar, Jahangir, **Shah** Jahan, and Aurangzeb—were all **patrons** of the arts, each with his own particular interests. Book illustration flourished, and many fine monuments were built, including the 17th-century **mausoleum,** the Taj Mahal.

The Mughal Empire declined after the death of Aurangzeb in 1707, as **Hindu** power reasserted itself and the British extended their **colonies.** It came to an end in 1858, when India was declared a British Crown Colony.

This beautiful dagger dates back to Mughal times. Its hilt (handle) is decorated with gold and **enamel** lotus leaf and flower motifs and set with rubies.

1526: Babur founds Mughal Empire. A great lover of books, he establishes the Mughal tradition of book illustration.

1627–58: Reign of Mughal ruler Shah Jahan. Taj Mahal is built as a memorial to his wife, Mumtaz Mahal.

1858: Fall of Mughal Empire. Declaration of India as a British Crown Colony.

1918: Collapse of Ottoman Empire. End of the last great Islamic empire.

Calligraphic tiles such as these are found on buildings throughout the Islamic world. Muslims avoid representations of living beings on religious buildings.

## Modern times

In 1798 French troops under Napoleon occupied Egypt. This marked the beginning of increasing European domination of Islamic countries. After the collapse of the Ottoman Empire, the republic of Turkey was founded in 1923. This was a **secular** state, with laws that did not openly refer to sacred texts. Iran also became a secular state under Riza Shah, who made himself **shah** in 1925.

After World War II, many former European colonies became independent, and in the Middle East states such as the United Arab Emirates, Qatar, and Bahrain were formed. Pakistan was founded in 1947 as a home for Muslims of the Indian subcontinent. In many of these states, people began to reject Western influences and to reassert the importance of Islam and its laws. In Iran, the Shah was overthrown in 1979 and replaced with Islamic church officials under the leadership of Ayatollah Khomeini.

In the 1990s, terrorism acted out by Islamic extremists became an increasing worldwide threat, often targeting the United States. U.S.-led coalitions invaded Afghanistan in 2001 and Iraq in 2003 as part of a newly declared "war on terror."

The impact of these and many other events on Islamic arts and crafts has been dramatic. With no royal patronage, cheap manufactured goods such as glass and pottery began to be imported from Europe, while Western styles also influenced many Islamic artists. However, many traditions have survived, most notably the art of **calligraphy.**

1925: Riza Shah founds Pahlawi dynasty in Iran.

1947: Founding of Pakistan.

1948: State of Israel founded, followed by first Arab–Israeli War.

1979: Revolution in Iran and overthrow of shah.

1980–88: Iran–Iraq War.

1991: Gulf War in response to Iraqi invasion of Kuwait.

2003: Coalition led by the United States and Great Britain invade Iraq. Threat to artifacts and archaeological monuments.

**11**

# Calligraphy

When the Prophet Muhammad received messages from God through the Angel Jibril, he memorized them. Later, it is said, he dictated them word for word to scribes (writers), who wrote them on various materials, such as pieces of bone and papyrus and bits of leather. After the death of Muhammad, a complete version of the messages from God was collected together to form the sacred book of Islam, the **Qur'an** (or Koran). The scribes wrote out the words in beautiful **calligraphy.** Muslims believe that not one word of the revelations was changed, and that the Qur'an is the actual word of God. Calligraphy is therefore the means by which the word of God is recorded and passed on and, as a result, it is considered the most precious and noble of all the Islamic arts.

## Arabic

The Qur'an was revealed in Arabic, the language of the first Muslims. The Arabs delighted in the spoken and written word, and poetry was a very important part of everyday life. Writing the words of the Qur'an was an act of worship on the part of the scribe, and great skill and care was, and is, taken in the creation of beautiful calligraphy worthy of the word of God.

These pages from an early Qur'an show the beautiful, flowing style of *naskhi* script.

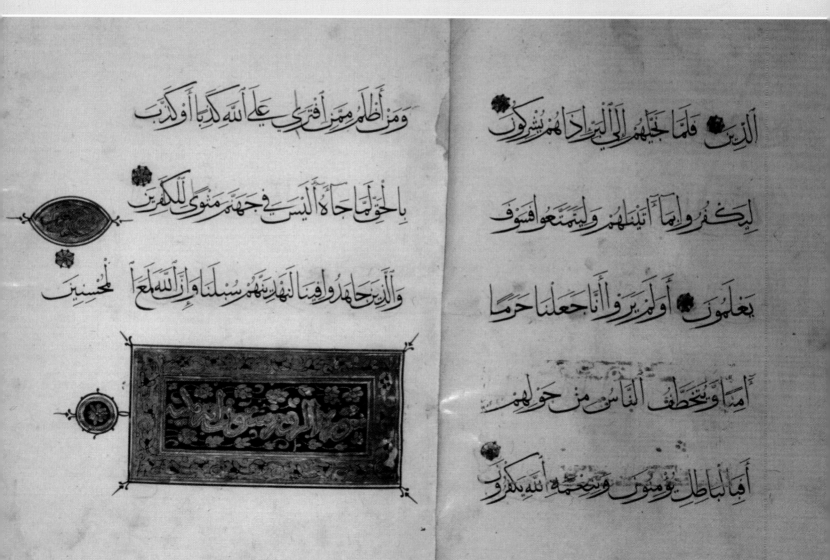

## ◈ Calligraphy tools

The tools of the calligrapher's trade have changed little over the centuries. They include reed and brush pens, scissors, a knife for cutting the pens, ink, and a sharpening tool. The reed pen, called a *qalam,* is used by many Islamic calligraphers. In the past, reed pens were valuable items traded across the Islamic world.

Calligraphers have a variety of pens of different thicknesses and learn to shape and sharpen them with a knife.

There are many recipes for inks, some colored, others perfumed. Traditionally, most were based on a mixture of soot or **lampblack,** water, and **gum arabic,** which is still used.

A girl practices her Arabic calligraphy at the annual Arab Festival of Arts, Mahrajan al-Fan, held in New York City. A woman in traditional Islamic dress watches her.

Different types of Arabic script have developed over the centuries. The earliest styles are often grouped together under the category kufic, which comes from an early center of calligraphy, Kufa, in Iraq. Kufic was an angular style, while *naskhi* was a more flowing (cursive) style. *Naskhi* was often used for **secular** writing, while kufic script was suited for ornamental use on buildings or pottery. In the 10th and 11th centuries, the famous calligraphers Ibn Muqlah and Ibn al-Bawwab established six different classical types of Arabic script: *naskhi, thuluth, muhaqqaq, rayhani, riqa,* and *tauqi.* These styles are still used by Islamic calligraphers today.

## Calligraphy as decoration

Throughout the history of Islamic art, **calligraphy** has been used for surface decoration in **mosques** and **madrasahs**, as well as on smaller objects such as tiles, plates, or mosque lamps (see page 35). Often, the text for the calligraphy is taken from the **Qur'an**. Calligraphy is used partly because of the importance that Muslims attach to the power of the word of God. But it is also a result of the Muslim tradition of avoiding the representation of living things on religious buildings and objects. There is no specific wording in the Qur'an that forbids this practice, but from the earliest times, Muslims did not use any such images to decorate their mosques.

## The Dome of the Rock

This tradition of not depicting living things can be seen in the earliest surviving Islamic monument and one of the holiest Islamic shrines: the Dome of the Rock in Jerusalem. The exterior is decorated with marble panels, beautiful **mosaics** in geometric patterns, and a panel of kufic script that runs around the entire building. The calligraphy is not only a beautiful surface decoration. Its text, taken from the Qur'an, also sends out a powerful message about the beliefs of Islam.

## Calligrams

Another development in the calligrapher's art was the calligram, a picture made from words that also have a symbolic meaning. The letters of the Arabic language have been shaped into boats, mosques, and even people and animals. The words for calligrams are often those of the Shahadah (the Muslim declaration of faith): "There is no god but God; Muhammad is the messenger of God."

## Modern calligraphy

Calligraphy continues to be an important part of Islamic culture today. Schools of calligraphy flourish in many Islamic countries, particularly Iran, Pakistan, and Turkey, with international competitions held annually. Some Islamic artists have pushed beyond the traditional boundaries to use calligraphy in new and individual ways. Examples include the work of the Iraqi calligrapher Hassan Massoudy and the Algerian artist Rachid Koraichi, who uses Islamic calligraphy together with Chinese and Japanese characters and other symbols to create **abstract** works of art.

### *Tugras*

A feature of calligraphy in the Ottoman Empire was the *tugra* (imperial seal) of the **sultan.** This was a kind of ornamental signature, made up of the name of the sultan and of his father, together with the words *ever victorious* The *tugra* was used on documents, coins, and **inscriptions** on buildings. *Tugras* were copied and heavily decorated for important documents. There is also evidence that stencils or stamps were used to reproduce *tugras* on the thousands of official documents that needed to carry the sultan's seal.

This *tugra* was created in 1575 for the Ottoman sultan Murad III.

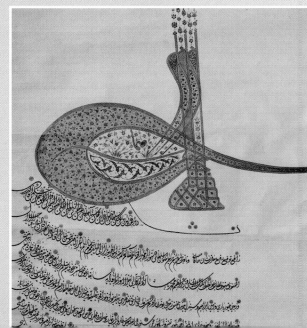

The outside of the **mausoleum** at the Taj Mahal in India is decorated with an inscription of verses from the Qur'an in beautiful, ornamental calligraphy and accompanied by panels of floral motifs. The inscription dates back to the 1630s.

# Book Illustration

The **Qur'an,** the sacred book of Islam, and other religious texts are never illustrated with depictions of living things, as we have seen. A separate tradition of illustrating **secular** texts with beautiful paintings developed in the Islamic world, although representations of the Prophet Muhammad and other holy men were also nearly always avoided within this context.

## Qur'an illumination

The earliest types of **illumination** to appear in copies of the Qur'an were decorative bands filled with geometric or floral patterns. These were used to separate verses and chapters in the text. This kind of illumination may have been used as early as the Umayyad period (661–750), but the oldest examples that survive date from the time of the Abbasids (750–1258).

## ◈ The paper revolution

In the 8th century, papermaking was introduced into the Islamic world. It is said that Chinese papermakers were among the prisoners captured during a battle in 751 between the Muslims and the Chinese. Before paper, vellum (fine parchment made from animal skin) was the most common material used for copies of the Qur'an. Paper was made from cotton, flax, or silk and was polished with a smooth stone to give a fine surface before the **calligrapher** began to write. Today, the best quality paper is usually used for printing Qur'ans.

These highly decorated pages are taken from a 14th-century Qur'an found in Damascus, Syria.

## Early books

While no pictures were ever used in copies of the Qur'an, other manuscripts were illustrated. The earliest illustrated books were often scientific works, where pictures were used to help explain the text. One of the oldest surviving examples is the *Book of the Fixed Stars,* which dates from the early 11th century. Based on the work of the ancient Greek astronomer Ptolemy, it shows the constellations (groups of stars) as human and animal forms. In time, other types of books began to be illustrated. One of the most popular was the *maqamah* ("assemblies") of al-Hariri, which related the adventures of a hero named Abu Zayd.

This village scene is taken from a copy of the *maqamah* of al-Hariri, illustrated in Baghdad in 1237. On the left, there is a mosque with a blue-tiled dome and a **minaret.** On the right, a figure is spinning yarn. In the foreground, the hero Abu Zayd talks to a man from the village.

As time went on, the decorative bands became wider and more elaborate, often containing the chapter titles. Decorations in the margins were also used to indicate different points in the text. From these early beginnings, Qur'an illumination became increasingly **opulent.** Whole pages of **intricate** patterns, often using a wide range of colored inks as well as gold, were placed at the beginning and end of the text.

In all the great Islamic empires, Muslim rulers commissioned beautiful Qur'ans as an indication not only of their religious faith but also of their wealth. For example, the Mamluks, who ruled Egypt from 1250 to 1517, were well known for buying large, beautifully decorated Qur'ans, which were often given to religious foundations such as **mosques** and *madrasahs.* Today, the need for handwritten and illuminated Qur'ans has been overtaken by the technology of printing. Qur'ans are printed at special printing houses such as the King Fahd Complex for Printing the Holy Qur'an in Saudi Arabia. Great care continues to be taken over the production of this sacred text.

## History books

Many early illustrated manuscripts were produced at the Abbasid capital, Baghdad. After the sack of Baghdad in 1258, however, the center of book illustration moved to Iran (Persia), which was under Mongol control. The Mongol rulers commissioned historical works such as Rashid al-Din's *Universal History* (1306–07), and the *Shahnama* ("History of the **Shahs**"), from about 1336. Rashid al-Din's book tells the history of the Islamic peoples, as well as the Mongols, Turks, Jews, Chinese, and Indians. The illustrations show a wide variety of influences, from Chinese scroll paintings to European Christian paintings. The *Shahnama* was a history of Persia before the arrival of the Muslims. It originally contained 200 large pictures, but only a quarter of this number survive.

## Portraits

During the reign of Shah Abbas I, artists began to produce works of art on single pages that could be sold separately. This practice continued over later centuries in the Mughal and Ottoman empires, as wealthy patrons collected single sheets in albums. These paintings were often portraits of people as well as pictures of animals, plants, and flowers. They were often signed by individual artists, unlike the paintings done for books at the Safavid court, which were usually unsigned. The most famous artist who worked for Shah Abbas was Riza Abbasi. He painted many portraits, often of ordinary people.

This painting comes from the *Shahnama*, a book created for Shah Tahmasp.

## Shah Tahmasp

Beautifully illustrated books were prized possessions at the courts of Islamic rulers, and during the 15th century Herat (in modern-day northwestern Afghanistan) became a center of book production. Certain texts became favorites for illustration, among them the *Shahnama* and the *Khamseh* ("Five Books") by Nizami, a 12th-century poet.

During the Safavid dynasty, Persian book production reached new heights, particularly under the **patronage** of Shah Tahmasp I. The *Shahnama* made for Shah Tahmasp was one of the most **sumptuous** Islamic books ever created. It had over 740 pages, more than 250 illustrations, and took 10 years to make. It was completed about 1535.

This beautiful illustration, showing Rudaba letting her hair down to help Zal climb up to her balcony, is taken from the *Shahnama*.

### ◈ Creating a book

A huge project, such as the *Shahnama* commissioned by Shah Tahmasp, required the talents of a wide range of people in the royal studio. **Calligraphers,** designers, painters, and bookbinders all worked together on such projects. The layout of the manuscript was decided first, before the calligrapher began to copy the text. When the text was in position, the painters started work. The artist first sketched in the outlines of the painting with thin, black ink. Then, colors were added, starting with gold and silver, followed by landscape and body colors, and ending with the fine details. For the final stage, the bookbinders gathered the pages together and sewed them into a leather binding.

## Painting at the Mughal court

The tradition of book production was continued by the Mughals. Under Akbar's rule, the royal studios employed more than 100 artists and had a huge output of illustrated books. Akbar's wide-ranging interests are reflected in the great variety of books produced during his reign. Persian translations of **Hindu epics** such as the *Mahabharata* and the *Ramayana* were produced, while popular classics of Persian literature such as the *Khamseh* of Nizami were also illustrated. Like the Mongols, Akbar also commissioned works of history, such as the *Akbarnama*, which chronicled the events of his own life. The illustrations are often finely detailed and patterned and feature brilliant, jewel-like colors. Mughal artists were also influenced by prints that came from Europe, and they began to use elements of shading and **perspective,** which were new to Islamic painting.

This 17th-century hunting scene is taken from the *Akbarnama*, the "History of Akbar." It shows Akbar surrounded by his followers and kneeling by his prey.

### ◈ Modern Islamic painting

During the 20th century, schools of painting were established in many Islamic countries, often as a result of contact with European styles and techniques. In Iran, Muhammad Ghaffari set up an art school after studying in Europe. He introduced painting on easels and used Western styles of perspective and light and shade in his work. Not all painters accepted European values, however. Some Iranian painters looked back to traditional Islamic styles, such as those seen in Timurid and Safavid miniatures. After the revolution in Iran in 1979, when the **shah** was overthrown, poster art became important as a way of showing support for the new revolutionary spirit in the country. It used a mixture of traditional and nationalistic styles.

## Maps and portraits

As the Ottoman world expanded in the 16th century, artists were brought back from all corners of the empire to work in Istanbul. These artists brought their own traditions, which were combined with the styles and interests of the Ottomans.

Like the Mughal emperors, the greatest Ottoman **sultan,** Sulaiman, commissioned a history of his own life, called the *Sulaimannama.* Some illustrations showed maps that were bird's-eye views of cities attacked or captured by the Ottomans on their campaigns. Another aspect of Ottoman painting was an interest in accurate portraits of individuals. This could also seen in the *Sulaimannama,* with careful representations of the sultan and his court.

## *The Thousand and One Nights*

Book illustration continued into the 19th century. The most notable example from this time was a huge project commissioned by Nasir al-Din, ruler of Iran, in the 1850s to illustrate the tales of *The Thousand and One Nights.* The court painter, Abu'l-Hasan Ghaffari, led a team of 34 painters. The book ran into 6 volumes, with a total of 1,134 pages, each with several illustrations. Ghaffari had studied in Italy, and the paintings show this Western influence in their startling and direct realism. Traditions of book illustration died out, however, as printing and the technique of lithography (printing from a stone or metal plate) replaced the labor-intensive work of illustration.

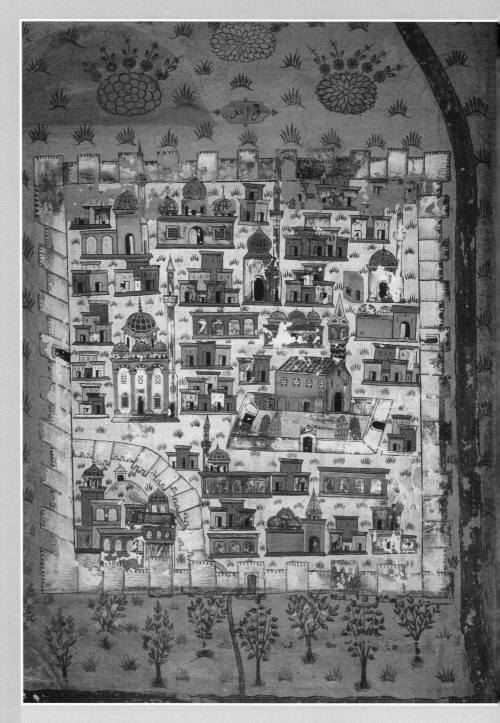

This bird's-eye view of the Turkish town of Diyarbakir was created by the Ottoman artist Nasuh al-Silahi in the 16th century. Diyarbakir was the scene of a revolt against Ottoman rule in the late 16th and early 17th centuries.

# Architecture

In the 7th century, Muslim armies invaded and conquered a huge expanse of land. Once the Muslims had taken control of a region, their first need was for a place to worship—a **mosque.**

## Early mosques

Mosques were built from the earliest days of Islam, and the first ones were based on the layout of the Prophet's Muhammad own house in Madinah. The house of the Prophet had a large central courtyard with deep porches to the north and the south. The north porch provided shelter from the sun for the homeless, while the south porch was for worshipers. The south wall indicated the *qiblah,* the direction of prayer toward Jerusalem. Later, the *qiblah* faced Makkah.

This simple layout provided the main elements that were to be incorporated into all mosques: an open space for prayer with some shelter from the weather and an indication of the *qiblah.*

At first, Muslims put up simple buildings based on the model of the Prophet's house or adapted existing buildings, such as churches, for their own worship. Then, under the Umayyads, the first great monuments of Islam were built.

The wall of the huge prayer hall in the courtyard of the Great Mosque of Damascus is decorated with mosaics.

## Jerusalem and Damascus

As the Muslims conquered the lands of the **Sassanians** and the **Byzantines** in the 7th century, they came across some well-established styles and methods of building. The Dome of the Rock in Jerusalem shows the influence of Byzantine buildings in its use of beautiful marble and **mosaics** on the walls, both inside and out. The Great Mosque of Damascus was built on the site of a Byzantine Christian church. Its layout is a large courtyard with a huge prayer hall along the south, or *qiblah*, wall. A new innovation was a semicircular **mihrab**, set into the *qiblah* wall. This quickly became popular throughout Islamic lands.

## Cordoba

The Great Mosque in Cordoba, Spain, is a reminder of the splendors of Muslim al-Andalus. Now a tourist attraction, it was begun during the reign of Abd al-Rahman (756–788). It shows the influence of Umayyad architecture in Syria, from which Abd al-Rahman had fled. For example, the beautiful mosaics in the Great Mosque, which date from the 10th century, were probably intended to equal the splendors of the mosaics on the Dome of the Rock in Jerusalem and the Great Mosque in Damascus. The workmen who made the mosaics came not from al-Andalus itself, nor from the Abbasid Empire, but from Constantinople, capital of the Byzantine Empire.

## The features of a mosque

Over time, extra features were added to the basic design of the mosque. The *minbar,* a type of stepped pulpit (a platform for preaching), was based on the high seat with three steps from which Muhammad talked to his followers. The mihrab is a niche set into the *qiblah* wall to indicate the direction of prayer. During the time of the Prophet Muhammad, the call to prayer, or *adhan,* was given from the roof of the house. Later, the **minaret,** a tall tower from which the *adhan* is called, was introduced.

This photograph was taken inside the Sokullu Mehmet Pasha Mosque in Istanbul, Turkey. You can see the highly decorated mihrab in the center and the *minbar* on the right.

The impressive mud walls of the Great Mosque in Djenne tower above the weekly open-air market.

## African styles

In the dry lands south of the Sahara, a distinctive style of **mosque** has developed that incorporates traditional aspects of mosque architecture with local building materials and styles. These mosques are made from sun-dried mud bricks, built around a wooden framework. The bricks are held together with mud and plastered over with more mud to give them a smooth surface. One of the best-known examples is in Djenne in Mali. Every year, a festival is held there during which thousands of people help to replaster the mosque walls with fresh mud.

## Types of mosque

Mosques are not only places of worship, but also community centers where food and shelter are available to those who need it. Many mosques also have areas for teaching and offices. Over the centuries, different types of mosques have developed, too. Everyday prayers can be performed anywhere, although many choose to do them in small mosques. The main prayer of the week, held on Friday, must be performed by all Muslim men in a mosque. At this meeting, an *imam* (Muslim leader) addresses the worshippers from the **minbar.** Large "Friday mosques" are usually at the center of Islamic towns and cities.

## Madrasahs

Over time, the different functions of the mosque separated, and new types of building emerged. **Madrasahs** are Islamic schools where students come to study the Islamic sacred texts and Islamic law. The first *madrasahs* were founded in the 10th century, and a large number were built by the Seljuks in Central Asia in the 11th century.

Traditionally, the layout of many *madrasahs* was, as in many mosques, based around a courtyard. In many Central Asian *madrasahs*, there was a large, open-air hall with an arched roof, called an **iwan,** on each of the four sides of the courtyard. Teachers and students lived in small rooms around the courtyard.

Today, the tradition of building *madrasahs* continues—for example, as part of the large complex of the Great Mosque of Hassan II in Morocco, completed in 1993.

## Tombs

Before his death, the Prophet Muhammad insisted that he should be buried very simply and his grave should not be marked. But as Islam spread, it inherited the burial traditions of other cultures, in which the graves of the dead were often marked with elaborate structures. The desire to commemorate the dead meant that tombs were built throughout the Islamic world, although they were regarded with mixed feelings by some Muslims.

Tombs were often cube-shaped, topped by a dome. Another style was the tomb tower, topped with a cone-shaped roof. Tombs of this design were built in northern Iran.

Tombs gradually became bigger and more decorated, reaching a high point in examples such as the Gur-i Amir, Timur's **mausoleum** in Samarkand, and the Taj Mahal built by the Mughal emperor **Shah** Jahan for his wife, Mumtaz Mahal.

## Modern mosques

In the modern era, architecture in most Islamic cities has become international in style. The exception is mosque architecture, which often retains traditional layout and features. However, these elements have also been combined with new materials and building techniques.

This mosque in Rome opened in 1992. Designed by the Italian architect Paolo Portoghesi, it combines traditional features such as the dome (shown right) with modern technology and materials.

The Topkapi Sarayi in Istanbul housed about 5,000 people, and the huge complex included parks, a parade ground, gardens, living quarters, and offices for government offices, as well as the sultan's private room.

## Palaces

From the Umayyad dynasty onward, Islamic rulers built **opulent** palaces for themselves. The Umayyads built palaces in the Syrian desert. The design of these palaces was a square enclosure surrounded by walls and containing living areas, baths, a small **mosque,** and a throne room. The palaces were decorated with carved **stucco** and **mosaics**.

The finest surviving example of palace architecture in western Islamic lands is the Alhambra in Granada, Spain. Granada was the last Muslim stronghold in Spain after the Christian kings began to reconquer the land in the 11th century. When Granada fell to the Christians in 1492, the Alhambra was preserved as a symbol of victory. The Alhambra is a group of palaces arranged around courtyards and elaborately decorated with wood, tiles, and carved plaster. The same rambling style of architecture is found in the Topkapi Sarayi, the palace of the Ottoman **sultans** in Istanbul.

## Everyday structures

Other types of structure found across the Islamic world include the caravanserais, the bazaar, and ordinary homes. Caravanserais were a type of motel situated along trade routes. Many had the same layout as was used for *madrasahs*: a large courtyard with an *iwan* on each side.

The bazaar (a market with rows of stalls) is the center of trade in many Muslim towns and cities. Most are roofed to provide some shelter from the hot sun. One of the largest is in the Safavid capital of Isfahan, where the alleys of the bazaar stretch for many miles.

The traditional Islamic home is based around a courtyard. The outside walls are either solid or have small windows. A single door leads into the men's rooms, where visitors are received, while the women's quarters, or harem, are separate. Many people still live in such houses, although Western-style houses and apartment blocks are also common in many Islamic cities.

## ◈ Gardens

In many parts of the Islamic world, gardens are highly prized. In places where the climate is hot and the landscape is **arid,** a lush, green garden with the sound of flowing water is seen as a kind of paradise. Indeed, references in the **Qur'an** to paradise describe it as a garden that features rivers and fountains. Many Persian and Mughal book illustrations show beautiful gardens, and gardens are important areas in palaces such as the Alhambra and the Topkapi Sarayi.

In the center of Isfahan, behind the Shah Mosque, is a huge open space called the Maydan. The Maydan was a space for markets, games of polo, military parades, and other state ceremonies.

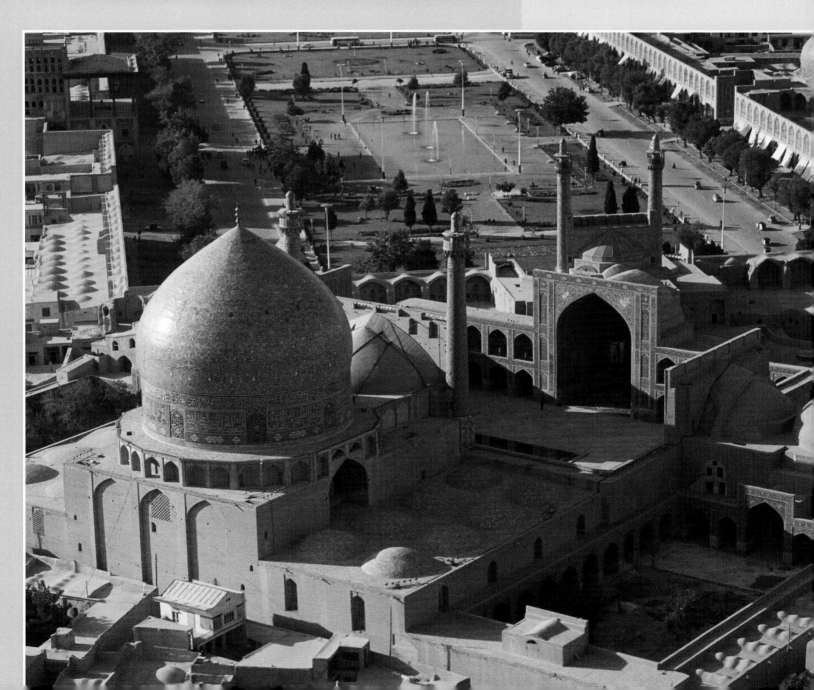

# Carving

From the earliest times, Islamic buildings have been decorated with **intricate** carving. Sometimes the carving is into the stone of the building itself, while at other times it is into a type of plaster called **stucco.** Some of the earliest surviving examples come from the Umayyad palaces built in the Syrian desert. For example, at Mshatta, the outside stone walls were decorated with elaborate carvings. These carvings include intricate loops of leaves, stems, and bunches of grapes arranged in large geometric shapes.

The carvings at Mshatta and at Khirbat al-Mafjar (another desert palace) show the influence of the great empires that went before the Islamic conquests: the ancient Greek and Roman worlds, the **Byzantine Empire,** and a Persian flavor from the **Sassanian Empire.** Byzantine and Sassanian artists had long used plant and geometric ornaments for decoration, while the animals and figures that decorate Khirbat al-Mafjar were based on Sassanian models.

## Abbasid carving

Nothing remains of the Abbasid capital at Baghdad. However, in the middle of the 9th century, when the Abbasids were forced to abandon Baghdad for a time, they built a new capital at Samarra. Evidence from archaeological digs at Samarra shows that the Abbasids used panels of stucco to decorate the inside walls of their palaces. Three different styles of stucco carving have been identified at Samarra. The first followed in the tradition of the Umayyad designs, the second used little dots across the surface of the stucco, and the third used slanted cuts in the plaster to create large, **abstract, symmetrical** designs. This last style quickly became popular across the Islamic world and was used not only for stucco decoration, but also for carving in wood, glass, and rock crystal.

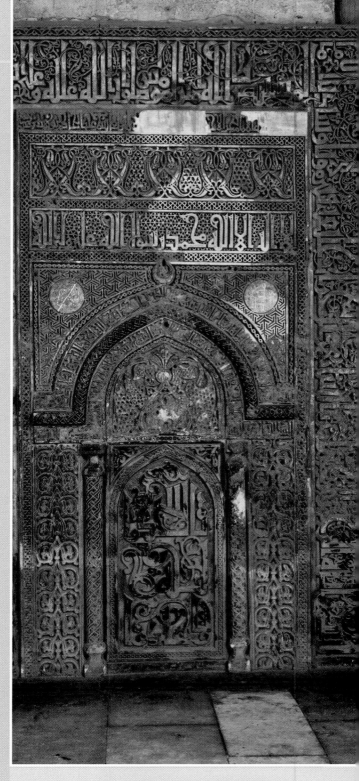

This beautifully carved stucco **mihrab** was added to the 9th-century **Mosque** of Ibn Tulun, in Cairo, in 1094. The **calligraphic inscriptions** are carved using the angular kufic style (see page 13).

## The Alhambra

Some of the finest stucco carving in the Islamic world has been preserved at the Alhambra Palace in Granada, Spain. The fine carving in the Court of the Lions gives a sense of weightlessness and light. In the Palace of the Lions there are two plaster ceilings featuring *muqarnas,* a style of ornament that hangs down like an icicle. This became a popular feature in Islamic architecture from the late 10th century onward.

This picture shows the beautiful stucco carving in the Court of the Lions, part of the Alhambra Palace in Granada, Spain.

### ◈ The arabesque

The designs used as surface decoration in much Islamic art are often based on motifs such as leaves, tendrils, and flowers. The abstract geometric patterns made from these motifs are known as **arabesque,** meaning "in the Arab style." Geometric patterns are a feature of art in the Islamic world, largely because of the tradition of avoiding the representation of living beings in religious contexts. Some patterns use arabesque styles, while others draw on simple forms such as the circle and the square.

## Woodwork

Carving in wood is closely related to carving for architectural decoration. Wood is used for **mosque** furniture as well as for doors, shutters, beams, screens, and other everyday furniture. The work is often extremely **intricate,** since it can be viewed and appreciated from close-up. Wood carving is still practiced as a local craft in many parts of the Islamic world.

The oldest surviving example of a wooden *minbar* is in the Great Mosque at Kairouan in Tunisia. Made in 862–63 from teak (a type of wood), it is thought that the carved panels may have been brought from Iraq. The panels have delicately carved designs, which have their origins in Umayyad and Abbasid ornament.

## Ivory

Carving in ivory often uses similar styles to carving in wood, but the work is usually of higher quality and more detailed. This is because ivory has always been an expensive material, treated with care and elegance. During the early Islamic period, ivory came from African elephant and hippopotamus tusks and was brought across the Sahara to Egypt and northern Africa. Some was exported to Cordoba in Spain (al-Andalus), which became particularly noted as a center for ivory carving. The ivory was used to make highly decorated containers. Only very wealthy **patrons** could afford such objects, and many containers have **calligraphic inscriptions** stating the owners' names. Ivory was also used in the Ottoman Empire to make small objects such as buckles and belts.

30

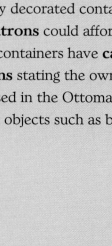

This detail shows the fine wood carving on an Egyptian **mihrab** dating from the 12th century.

## Jade

Another precious and highly prized material is jade. This hard stone is white or green, and during the time of the great Islamic empires it was imported from Central Asia and East Asia. Drinking from a jade cup was thought to cure digestive complaints, and it was believed that a jade cup would break if it came into contact with poison. Carving in jade was particularly associated with the Timurids. Later, Mughal emperors drank only from cups made of jade or gold. Cups were often carved in a Chinese style, with handles shaped like small dragons.

The 17th-century Mughal emperor **Shah Jahan** owned this jade cup.

## ◈ Papier mâché

Papier mâché is a material made from a mixture of paper and glue. It can be molded or built up on a frame. When it hardens, it is both light and surprisingly strong. This material was used to decorate the inside of the Gir-i Amir ("Lord's Tomb") in Samarkand. It was built for Timur and was the site of his burial in 1405. The papier mâché was molded and sculpted and then painted to decorate the vaults inside the tomb. This is one of the first known uses of this material in a building. Today, papier mâché is used for traditional crafts, such as trays, boxes, and other items made in Kashmir, in the far north of India. The surfaces of these objects are painted with floral designs in jewel-like colors, usually on a dark background.

# Rock Crystal and Glass

Rock crystal is a type of quartz (a transparent, colorless stone) used in the Islamic world to make beautiful bowls, **ewers,** and cups. Rock crystal was highly prized by the Fatimids. Indeed, thousands of rock crystal objects were made for the **opulent** Fatimid court. The Fatimids imported rock crystal from Arabia and Iraq, as well as from East Africa. Rock crystal was also a favorite of the Ottoman **sultans,** who commissioned elaborate pieces that were often encrusted with precious stones such as emeralds and rubies.

## Magical properties

One reason that rock crystal was popular in the Islamic world was that crystal cups are mentioned in the **Qur'an** in association with paradise. But rock crystal was also thought to have other, magical properties. Drinking from a rock crystal cup was believed to prevent nightmares and to protect against some illnesses. It was also thought that rock crystal, like jade, would shatter if it came into contact with poison. Although most of the surviving pieces of rock crystal are objects such as bowls or cups, other items were made from the material. A crescent-shaped piece of rock crystal, with an **inscription** of the Fatimid ruler al-Zahir, was probably mounted on the harness of the **Khalifah's** horse. It would have flashed and sparkled beautifully in the sunlight.

## Making glass

The tradition of making objects from glass was well established in Egypt, Syria, Iraq, and Iran by the 7th century. Islamic glassmakers refined and developed new glass technologies. Glass was made from sand and lime, which was heated to a high temperature. It was shaped by being poured into molds or by blowing. This involved placing a lump of molten (melted) glass on the end of a long tube. The glassmaker then blew down the tube, creating a hollow shape in the glass. In some modern workshops, glass is still made in this traditional manner. However, glass production in the Islamic world declined after the 19th century, with the introduction of factory-produced European glass. European factories even made special designs for the Middle Eastern markets based on traditional Islamic wares. In the 20th century, glass-making techniques were revived in Egypt. Today, factories in Cairo produce blown glass made from recycled bottles.

## ◈ Carving rock crystal

Rock crystal is a very hard and brittle substance. Great skill was required to hollow it out without shattering or blemishing it. The outside surface was decorated by cutting away at the crystal with a rough material mounted on a turning wheel.

This ewer was carved out of a solid piece of rock crystal in the 10th century. Made for the Fatimid court, it is decorated with birds.

## Decorating glass

Islamic glassmakers continued the traditions of decorating glass that had been practiced in the **Byzantine** and **Sassanian empires.** Glass could be decorated before it had cooled and hardened by pushing molds into the soft glass to leave an impression or by pinching and shaping the glass with tools. Glass could also be blown into a decorative mold. Sometimes, threads of hot glass were poured onto the outside of the object to create spiral effects. Hard glass was scratched with an even harder point, such as a diamond, or cut and ground with a wheel. Glass could also be colored.

This 7th-century glass bottle from Syria is decorated with spiral patterns and covered with a luster glaze.

Many glass objects were simple undecorated objects, designed for everyday use. These were usually made by the blown-glass method. Other pieces were beautifully decorated and were obviously made for wealthy **patrons.** Several cut-glass beakers survive from Fatimid Egypt. Some have decorations very similar to those seen on the **stucco** wall of Samarra, while others are engraved with pictures of lions, eagles, and **griffins.**

## Luster glazes

The technique of decorating glass with **glazes** containing metallic **pigments** was probably developed in Egypt in the 7th century. These glazes are known as **luster** glazes because they give off a metallic shine. The use of luster glazes quickly spread to pottery and became an important method of **ceramic** decoration.

Richly decorated glass was a speciality in Egypt and Syria during the 13th and 14th centuries. Ayyubid and Mamluk glassmakers used both luster and **enamel** to decorate their wares. Red enamel was used to outline the shapes of the decorations, which were then filled in with luster and with white, yellow, green, blue, purple, or pink enamels. Decorated bottles, goblets, bowls, and vases were made not only for wealthy patrons, but also for sale and export, and they influenced the famous glassmakers in Venice, Italy. However, the object most commonly associated with Mamluk glassmakers was the **mosque** lamp (see page 35).

## Mosque lamps

Thousands of richly decorated lamps were made for the mosques of the Mamluk capital in Cairo and for Damascus in Syria. Typically, such lamps were decorated with **calligraphic inscriptions.** Often, these inscriptions gave the name of the **sultan** who had commissioned them, as well as a verse from the **Qur'an.** These 14th-century mosque lamps are made of enameled glass.

# Metalwork

Over the centuries, different traditions of metalworking developed in various parts of the Islamic world. Wealthy **patrons** paid for elaborate items to display their importance and power, and beautiful objects such as plates were often given as gifts. Less luxurious metals, most commonly brass, were used to make objects such as **ewers,** buckets, incense burners, bottles, candlesticks, and lamps. However, in the 19th century, factory-made items from Europe began to be imported into the Islamic world, and craft industries such as metalworking suffered as a result. Nevertheless, local traditions of metalworking continue in many Islamic countries, supplying both locals and the tourist industry.

## Early metalwork

Metalworking was well known throughout the Middle East from ancient times. Gold, silver, copper, iron, zinc, and lead were all mined in areas of the Islamic world. Iron and steel (iron and carbon) were used to make weapons and armor. But brass (usually copper and zinc) was the most common alloy (mixture of two metals), used for everyday items and as the base material for more luxurious objects. It is still the most widely used metal today.

Gold and silver were more costly and therefore used to make precious objects, such as luxury tableware, fine jewelry, and coins. However, few objects made from gold and silver survive from early Islamic times because the metal was so valuable that the objects were often melted down to be reused. Those items that have survived are mostly from treasure buried but never reclaimed.

## Working metal

Many examples of early Islamic metalwork were made using molds. However, the more common method of working metal was by beating or hammering a sheet of metal into shape, a technique that is still widely used today. Hollow metal objects were also made by spinning on a lathe, a special rotating machine. A disc of metal was attached to a lathe and spun rapidly. It was then shaped by pressing a piece of shaped wood against the metal. The earliest known examples of this technique date from the 13th century.

### ◆ Forbidden metals

Although gold and silver have been highly prized throughout the Islamic world, the sacred texts of Islam warn against these precious metals. The **Qur'an** condemns the hoarding (storing or hiding away) of gold and silver. The *Hadith* (the collected sayings of the Prophet Muhammad, which are a source of Islamic law and tradition) says: "He who drinks from a silver vessel will have hellfire gurgling in his belly." This may explain the popularity through the centuries of **inlaid** brass, which has the luxurious appearance associated with gold and silver while remaining within Islamic religious law.

These metalworkers in Indonesia are making stars and crescents—symbols of Islam—for **mosques.**

## Herat and Mosul

The 10th century saw the beginning of an age of fine metalwork in the Islamic world. One of the main centers of production was Herat (in modern-day northwest Afghanistan). Brass was still used as the main metal for most metal objects, but it was transformed by the technique of **inlaying** more precious metals, such as silver, red copper, or gold. The effect was one of great **opulence** and luxury, with metal objects covered in **arabesque** and geometric designs.

One of the best-known examples of this work is the Bobrinsky bucket (its name comes from the Russian collector who bought it). It is made of brass and inlaid with silver and copper in horizontal bands that alternate Arabic **inscriptions** and scenes from everyday life. Other objects from the workshops in Herat include **intricate** candlesticks, also inlaid with silver and copper. They have designs that were made by hammering the brass from the inside, so that the ornament stands out from the outside surface.

After the Mongol invasions of the 13th century, Mosul (in northern Iraq) emerged as an important center of metalworking. Designs and techniques mastered in Mosul spread to other parts of the Islamic world, including Syria. A flask from Syria shows that Islamic craftworkers were making goods not only for Muslim customers, but also for Christian **patrons.** The flask is decorated in Mosul style, but with Christian images, including the Virgin and Child and the Nativity (the scene of Christ's birth).

This 13th-century Persian **ewer** is made from brass. Its surface is finely decorated with inlaid silver in intricate patterns.

## Ottomans and Mughals

In the Ottoman Empire, interest in fine metalworking grew during the 16th century. This probably reflected the fact that it was the practice for **sultans** to be trained in a craft, and both Selim I and Suleiman I learned goldsmithing.

A feature of Ottoman metalwork was the use of jewels such as ruby, emerald, and turquoise set into the metal body of an object. Jewels were used to decorate a wide range of items, from weapons to mirrors. The Mughals also loved richly decorated metalwork, particularly weapons such as daggers, to display their wealth.

The creation of metal goods continues today in countries such as Iran and Pakistan. Metalworkers still use many of the traditional decorative techniques, including inlaying and **embossing,** which are centuries old. Some fine pieces are made entirely by hand, while others are die-cast, a process in which the melted metal is poured into a mold that is removed once the metal has cooled. Brass is still widely used to make objects for everyday use as well as decorative items. In Iran, there are local traditions of making certain metalwork items, including buckles, jewelry, and weapons.

### ◈ Jewelry

Metal has been used throughout the Islamic world to make jewelry, most often silver and gold. In North Africa, a common feature of Islamic jewelry is the *khamsa,* or "hand of Fatima." This is a hand-shaped charm, often with an eye on the back of the hand, named after the daughter of the Prophet Muhammad. It is meant to ward off the evil eye, a look that is thought to be able to cause pain or harm. The most common type of jewelry in Morocco is the *tizara,* a necklace made from gold coins, pearls, and jewels.

Door knockers are still made in the shape of the hand of Fatima, a good-luck symbol that is meant to ward off evil spirits.

# Pottery

The use of clay to make **ceramics** was well established by the time of the Muslim conquests in the 7th century. Clay is a type of very fine earth found along riverbanks. Together with sand and water, it was formed into simple earthenware pots that were used to carry and store water and food. Various methods of making pottery have developed since those early days. The clay can be shaped with the hands as it turns rapidly on a wheel, it can be pressed or poured into a mold, or it can be built up in coils and slabs. Whatever method is used, it is then left to dry before being baked in a special furnace, called a **kiln.**

## ◈ William De Morgan

Techniques of applying luster glazes were revived during the Safavid period in the late 17th and early 18th centuries, but then fell into disuse. In the 19th century, a British artist named William De Morgan was inspired by the beauty of Persian luster pottery from Kashan, which he saw in new collections in London museums. He began experiments to try to recreate the effects of luster and soon produced copper-red, gold, and silver lusters.

This Turkish potter is using a wheel to make a fine vase.

Earthenware is porous, meaning it can absorb water and air. Potters discovered that by painting a thin, glassy substance, called a **glaze,** onto the surface of pots, they could make them waterproof. The glaze could also be colored, allowing for simple decoration of the pot.

## Early developments

The earliest pottery of the Islamic lands was simple and practical, but potters soon began to experiment with new techniques and designs. Great developments in pottery were made under the Abbasids. Different colored glazes were combined to make patterns, and **luster** glazes were developed. The use of **calligraphy** to decorate pottery was also introduced. But, in particular, Abbasid potters were influenced by the designs of Chinese ceramics, which began to be imported to the Abbasid court during the 8th century. China was to remain a major influence on Islamic pottery for many centuries to come.

## Lusterware

Luster glazes had been used to decorate glass since the 7th century, but the technique was adapted for ceramics by Abbasid potters. At first, the luster glaze was painted across the whole vessel to give a smooth, metallic sheen. But from about 850, Abbasid potters began to experiment with increasingly complex designs in different colored lusters. These designs featured animals or humans, often surrounded by **abstract** patterns.

Lusterware was popular with the Fatimids, who ruled Egypt from the 10th to the 12th centuries. This gold lusterware plate shows a seated figure holding two cups.

## Kashan

In the late 12th century, a new pottery technique developed, possibly at Kashan in western Iran. A type of body material was made from quartz, which was ground and mixed with white clay and a ground **glaze** called frit. Fritware, as it was called, was fine and white and could be formed into delicate, elegant shapes. Once again, it was inspired by the Islamic potters' desire to copy Chinese porcelainware. Other techniques that were developed at Kashan included lusterware and **enameled ceramics** called *minai* (from the Persian word for enamel). Both of these techniques were used to produce high-quality luxury goods.

In addition to bowls, plates, and other similar items usually associated with ceramics, the Kashan potters also worked on a larger scale. **Mihrabs** made entirely from large panels of ceramic were made for **mosques.** The mihrabs were covered with **luster** glaze and decorated with **calligraphic inscriptions.**

## Iznik

From the 15th century, production of high-quality blue-and-white pottery centered on Iznik in northwestern Anatolia (Turkey), part of the expanding Ottoman Empire. After the Safavid defeat at the Battle of Chaldiran in 1514, Iranian artists were brought to work in the royal studios in Istanbul. Their influence is shown in designs including the Iranian *saz* style, which features delicately curving leaves with feathered edges.

The peak of achievement by the Iznik potters came in the second half of the

This fritware plate comes from Iznik. It has been painted and then glazed.

## Underglaze painting

The development of fritware led to a new technique of underglaze painting. This meant that the design was painted directly onto the body of the object, and then a clear glaze was applied over the top. Using this technique, potters created designs that were influenced by Chinese examples, often using blue motifs against the white background of the body material.

16th century. New colors had been added to the blue and white—usually black, green, and purple. A red **pigment** called Iznik red was developed during the 1550s. Iznik designs became extremely popular across Europe, and they were exported abroad, in addition to being imitated in potteries in Italy and Hungary. The popularity of Iznik declined during the 18th century.

Kutahya is a well-known center for ceramic production in modern-day Turkey. This woman is painting a ceramic jar with a fine brush.

Ceramics are still produced in local workshops in countries such as Iran and Pakistan, often using traditional designs and methods of working. The knowledge that is kept alive in such places is important when a building is being restored or when tiles are needed for a new construction. More large-scale production is found in Turkey, but Iznik continues to make pottery in traditional styles, mainly for export overseas. In the late 19th century, William De Morgan (see page 40) was invited by the Egyptian government to revitalize the ceramics industry, and he oversaw the establishment of a ceramics factory in Cairo. However, the outstanding figure in Egyptian ceramics in the 20th century was an Egyptian, Said al-Sadr. He trained in Great Britain, but studied the rich heritage of Islamic pottery and championed the study of ceramics in Egypt. He set up a ceramics center and established a mixture of traditional and modern styles, looking back at old styles but making use of up-to-date techniques.

# Tiles

The manufacture of tiles to provide color and decoration on buildings has long been one aspect of the art of the Islamic world. Both inside and outside walls are covered with **glazed** and unglazed tiles, usually highly decorated. While the actual structures of early Islamic buildings were often quite simple, their decoration became increasingly elaborate, particularly in the eastern lands of the Islamic world.

This Moroccan tilemaker is at work on a mosaic tile. Examples of his work are displayed on the wall.

## Ottoman tilework

Magnificent panels of tiles were made for the Ottoman **sultans** at the pottery workshops in Iznik in Turkey. The decoration on these tiles often used floral designs and the *saz* designs (see page 42) seen on pottery and Ottoman **textiles.** The interior of the Baghdad Kiosk in the Topkapi Palace in Istanbul is beautifully decorated with tilework showing the range of motifs and colors used by Ottoman tileworkers. In addition to floral and geometric motifs, there is a panel of calligraphy. Today, tiles are still made in Iznik and are exported all over the world.

## Decorative techniques

Just as in pottery, different techniques have been developed over the centuries to decorate tiles. **Luster** glazes were often used for tiles that decorated inside walls, turning them into sheets of gold or silver. Another method, known as *lajvardina*, made use of a blue glaze ornamented with red and white **enamel** and gold leaf. Other techniques allowed the use of several different colors on a tile without their running into one another. *Lakabi* was a style of decoration with raised ridges to separate different colors. In *cuerda seca* ("dry cord"), a type of greasy black paste was used to separate the colors. When the tiles were fired in a **kiln,** the paste burned off, leaving a black line between the colors.

There are several different styles for the decorative designs on tiles. Geometric designs are particularly associated with the tilework of northern Africa. Elsewhere, geometric designs are combined with **arabesque** and floral ornament. **Calligraphic inscriptions** are an important decoration, too.

Tiles are made in several different ways. Sometimes they are cut into shapes to form a **mosaic** pattern. Sometimes individual tiles form part of the larger pattern of a complete panel. In some cases, tiles are carved to form **intricate** decorative latticework (designs using a framework of crossed strips). Glazed wall tiles continue to be made in many Islamic countries, often using modern production techniques.

## The Shah Mosque, Isfahan

Some of the most magnificent examples of tilework in the Islamic world are found in cities such as Isfahan and Samarkand. In Isfahan, the **Shah Mosque** is covered in beautiful multicolored tilework, although the overall effect is blue. The most highly ornamented tilework is around the entrance to the mosque, where there are large panels of decorated tiles. Other parts of the mosque are less **sumptuously** decorated, probably due to shortage of money, in multicolored glazed tiles.

The interior of the Baghdad Kiosk in the Topkapi Palace in Istanbul is elaborately decorated with beautiful tilework featuring floral and geometric motifs as well as a panel of calligraphy.

# Textiles and Carpets

For centuries, the production and use of **textiles** has been very important across the Islamic world. Textiles have been used to make clothing, carpets, bags, tents, and furniture. The tradition of weaving tents originated with the **nomadic** tribes of the Islamic world: the Bedouin Arabs, the Turkomans, and the Mongols. In Muslim houses, carpets are spread on the floor and hung on walls to protect against extremes of temperature, while large woven bags are used for storage and cushions are used for sitting.

## Materials

The importance of textiles is shown by the number of textile-related words that have passed down into the English language from Arabic or Persian origins: the word *damask* comes from Damascus, the capital of Syria; *muslin* from Mosul in Iraq; and *taffeta* from *tafteh*, the Persian word for "woven." The most common material in use from early to modern times is sheep's wool. Other materials are goat and camel hair, cotton, linen, flax, and, the most expensive of all, silk, which is made from the cocoons of silkworms. Silk is spoken of in the **Qur'an** as one of the luxuries to be enjoyed in paradise.

Many textiles made for everyday use are plain, but patterned textiles are also very popular. For the most **sumptuous** effect, the pattern is woven into the cloth as it is made on the loom. Patterns are also added after the cloth is made by dying, printing, painting, or embroidery. Traditions of producing luxurious cloth largely died out from the 19th century, as Islamic rulers adopted Western dress. However, carpets are still made in many places using traditional methods.

## Early examples

Very few textiles from early Islamic times have survived to the present day. Some have been found in archaeological digs, including the oldest-known example of a hand-knotted wool carpet. Known as the Pazyryk carpet, it dates back to the pre-Islamic era of the 4th and 5th centuries B.C.E. The carpet was found virtually intact in southern Siberia, preserved in the frozen chamber of a royal burial mound. It is now kept at the Hermitage Museum in St. Petersburg, Russia. Other pieces of fabric were taken from the Islamic world to Europe as trophies. They were so highly regarded that they were often preserved in church treasuries, wrapped around precious relics, and have therefore survived until the present day.

## Kilims

A kilim is a kind of flat-woven carpet or hanging. Produced in many Islamic countries, from northern Africa to Turkey and the Middle East, these flat-woven fabrics were originally created to make saddlebags for animals, sacks, furnishings, and floor coverings. Kilims are traditionally died with vegetable dyes to produce bright colors. Designs vary from region to region, but they are often bold, with geometric patterns. Today, Turkey specializes in arch (**mihrab**) designs, which are popular in many non-Islamic countries.

This Turkish woman is repairing a brightly decorated kilim.

## Persian carpets

Knotted carpets were once made across the Islamic world. Examples survive from Konya and Ushak in Anatolia, Cairo in Egypt, and Islamic Spain. In the 16th century, Safavid Iran became an important center of carpet production. Under **Shah** Tahmasp and Shah Abbas, royal factories were set up for the manufacture of fine-quality carpets. Thousands of carpets were made for local use and for export to Europe, the Ottoman Empire, and India. Persian carpets are still very popular, and there are centers of manufacture in Iran. Each has its own unique designs and methods of production.

## Ottoman textiles

Just like the Safavids, the Ottomans also set up royal workshops for the production of fine **textiles** and carpets. The Ottoman **sultans** wore simple robes called caftans, which were made from **sumptuous** patterned silk and velvets. For military campaigns, the Ottoman sultans used large tents, often decorated with beautiful **appliqué** designs. There was also a fine tradition of carpet making, using both wool and silk.

## The DOBAG project

During the 19th century, traditional methods of carpet making were replaced by techniques more focused on making money in many parts of the Islamic world. Synthetic (human-made) dyes were used instead of traditional plant dyes, and carpet production moved into factories. Nevertheless, the tradition of producing hand-knotted carpets did not completely die out, and fine wool carpets and kilims are still made for home use and for export. In some places, projects have been set up to revive traditional techniques and provide fair

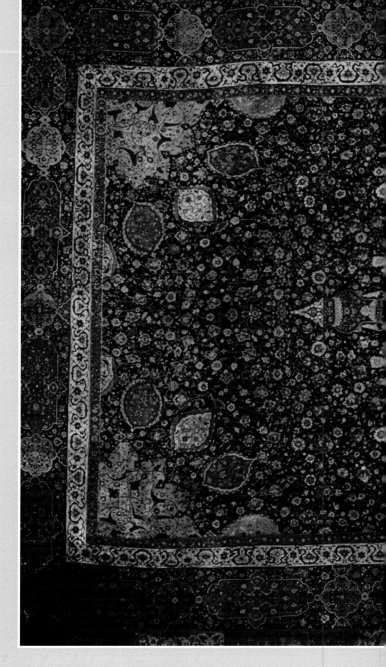

employment for carpet makers. One example is the DOBAG project in Turkey. DOBAG stands for the Turkish words for Natural Dye Research and Development Project, and the project is run by the University of Marmara. Begun in 1982, this is the first women's rug-weaving cooperative in the Islamic world. The women make the rugs in their own homes, using only vegetable dyes to color the wool. The designs of the rugs are unique and have been passed down through families over generations.

## ◇ Carpet knots

## Carpet knots

Carpets are traditionally made by hand, by knotting pieces of wool around the backing yarns. Two different knots are used to make carpets in the Islamic world. The Turkish, or Ghiordes, knot is a **symmetrical** knot. It is generally used for carpets made in Turkey and the Caucasus (between the Black and Caspian seas). The Persian, or Senneh, knot is an asymmetrical (not symmetrical) knot. It is associated with carpets from Iran and parts of Asia.

The Ardabil carpet (above) was woven in Persia between 1539 and 1540. It is made from wool and silk, and its design incorporates two **mosque** lamps (see page 35) hanging from the central medallion.

# Crosscurrents

The term *Islamic art* covers a wide range and huge variety of cultures. There are great differences, for example, in styles of architecture in Muslim Spain and Mughal India, although both were Islamic empires. Yet there are also features that make Islamic art and architecture recognizably Islamic in any part of the world: the use of **calligraphy,** for example, or the use of geometric and **arabesque** designs.

## Islam meets Hinduism

The most celebrated emperor of the Mughal Empire, Akbar, took a great interest in all religions. In the 1580s he even declared a new religion, which blended aspects of Islam with **Hinduism** and other faiths. The buildings commissioned by Akbar reflect this mixing of Islamic and local Hindu ideas. Akbar's most spectacular architectural achievement was Fatehpur Sikri, near Agra, which he began building in 1571 as a new capital for his empire. It was abandoned in the 1580s, but the buildings still stand today. The city is built from red sandstone, and the design combines Hindu styles and decorations with Islamic features.

## Islam in Southeast Asia

Islam was taken to Southeast Asia by sailors who crossed the Indian Ocean in search of trade. Conversion to Islam was slow and patchy, but by 1500, Muslims were established in many parts of the region, particularly Sumatra and Java. The traditions of Islam mixed with local cultures, as well as the Hindu and **Buddhist** religions, which also thrived in the region. For example, in Java, craftspeople produced **batik** cloth that was richly patterned with many different designs, including butterflies, birds, and flowers. In areas where Islam was strongest, representations of living beings were replaced by the geometric patterns developed by Muslim artists.

This **textile** worker in Java, Indonesia, is at work on a piece of batik cloth. He is applying hot wax to the fabric using a press. When the fabric is dipped in dye, the areas covered in wax will not be colored. The wax is removed by boiling the cloth.

## Islam and the West

In the West, there has long been an awareness of the riches of the Islamic world. From as early as the 1450s, paintings by European artists depict **sumptuous** carpets with distinctive patterns that show their origins in the Islamic workshops of Turkey (Anatolia). In the 16th century, Hans Holbein, court painter to Henry VIII, included beautiful carpets in his portraits of court figures. However, it was during the 18th century that interest in Islamic art and architecture began to take off, as European visitors to Turkey told of the wonders they had seen there. Islamic monuments such as the Taj Mahal at Agra, in India, inspired European architects who incorporated Islamic elements into their work. In the 19th century, the English poet and designer William Morris took inspiration from the patterns of carpets from Persia and Turkey for his own work. Exhibitions of Islamic art were mounted in Europe during the 19th century, exciting great interest and influencing painters such as Henri Matisse.

### ◈ Matisse

The French painter Henri Matisse visited several exhibitions of Islamic work and traveled to Morocco in northern Africa and Cordoba and Granada in Spain. Inspired by what he saw, he incorporated elements from Islamic art into his painting. His use of bright, jewel-like colors, new patterns, and a flattening of **perspective** all drew on his knowledge of Persian manuscript paintings and other Islamic work. His interest in the Islamic world continued throughout his life.

The Royal Pavilion in Brighton, England, was redesigned and rebuilt between 1815 and 1822 by the British architect John Nash. Its style reflects the growing interest in Islamic art and architecture of the time.

# Further Resources

## More books to read

DuTemple, Lesley A. *The Taj Mahal.* Minneapolis, Minn.: Lerner Publishing Group, 2002.

Egan, Andrew. *Islam.* Chicago: Raintree, 2003.

Mantra Publishing. *Journey Through Islamic Art.* Aurora, Ill.: Mantra Publishing, 2004.

Marston, Elsa. *The Byzantine Empire.* Tarrytown, N.Y.: Benchmark Books, 2002.

Martell, Hazel Mary. *The World of Islam Before 1700.* Chicago: Raintree, 1998.

Morris, Neil. *The Atlas of Islam.* Hauppauge, N.Y.: Barron's Educational Series, 2003.

Penney, Sue. *Islam.* Chicago: Heinemann Library, 2000.

Ruggiero, Adriane. *The Ottoman Empire.* Tarrytown, N.Y.: Benchmark Books, 2002.

## Using the Internet

Explore the Internet to find out more about Islamic art and culture.
Have an adult help you use a search engine. Type in a keyword,
such as *mosques, calligraphy,* or *lusterware.*

# Places to visit

## United States

Ackland Art Museum, Chapel Hill, North Carolina

Arthur M. Sackler Museum, Harvard University, Cambridge, Massachusetts

Brooklyn Museum of Art, New York

Detroit Institute of Arts, Michigan

Freer and Sackler Galleries, Smithsonian Institution, Washington, D.C.

Indianapolis Museum of Art, Indiana

Los Angeles County Museum of Art, California

Metropolitan Museum of Art, New York City

Minneapolis Institute of Arts Museum, Minnesota

Philadelphia Museum of Art, Pennslyvania

Virginia Museum of Fine Arts, Richmond

# Glossary

**abstract**   art that does not imitate the way the world around us looks

**appliqué**   technique of sewing pieces of fabric and other elements, such as beads, onto a fabric background to create an image

**arabesque**   meaning "in the Arab style," a form of surface decoration that uses abstract geometric patterns made up of motifs such as flowers

**arid**   very dry climate in which there is not enough rainfall for plants to grow

**batik**   technique of printing on fabric using wax

**Buddhism**   widespread Asian religion and philosophy

**Byzantine Empire**   empire of Byzantium, the eastern Roman Empire. It dated from 330 C.E., when the Roman emperor Constantine moved his capital to Byzantium and renamed it Constantinople (now Istanbul).

**calligraphy**   art of beautiful writing

**ceramic**   material that is shaped and then hardened by firing. Is is usually used for pottery, but also with other materials, such as enamel.

**colony**   territory occupied and ruled by another country

**embossing**   type of decoration that is pushed out from the inside, standing apart from the outside surface of an ornament

**enamel**   metallic compound that can be fired to produce glossy, colored decoration

**epic**   long poem that tells a story

**ewer**   large jug, often with a lid

**glaze**   glossy coating often applied to pottery when it is being fired

**griffin**   winged monster with the head of an eagle and the body of a lion

**gum arabic**   gum obtained from the acacia tree. It is used as a thickener in many products, including ink.

**Hinduism**   major religious and cultural tradition of India. Hindus worship many gods and goddesses and believe that a person is reborn many times into many different lives.

**illumination**   elaborate decoration on a manuscript

**inlay**   small piece of material, such as ivory or jade, that is inserted into an object or decoration

**inscription**   words that have been engraved or written on an object

**intricate**   complex

*iwan*   arched roof

**Ka'bah**   cube structure in Makkah toward which all Muslims direct their prayers.

*Khalifah*   title given to the successors of the Prophet Muhammad

**kiln**   big furnace in which pottery can be fired

**lampblack** black powder made from carbon, it is used as a pigment

**luster** type of glaze that contains a metallic pigment

*madrasah* Islamic school or college

**mausoleum** large tomb

**mihrab** niche in the wall of a mosque that indicates the *qiblah* (direction of prayer) toward Makkah

**minaret** tall tower from which the *adhan* (call to prayer) is given

*minbar* platform in a mosque from which the address is given during Friday prayers

**mosaic** form of decoration made by inlaying small pieces of colored materials to make a design

**mosque** place where Muslims worship. It comes from the Arabic *masjid*, meaning "a place of bowing down."

**nomadic** describes people who move from one place to another without a permanent home, usually in search of grazing land for their flocks

**oasis** area with water in the midst of dry desert

**opulent** indicating great wealth

**patron** someone who pays an artist for a specific piece of work

**perspective** way an artist draws objects in space, in order to suggest their size and how near or far away the objects are

**pigment** substance that gives something color

*qiblah* direction of prayer toward Makkah

**Qur'an** holy book of Islam, sacred to all Muslims

**Sassanian Empire** empire of the Sassanids, a Persian dynasty, from the 3rd to the 7th centuries. At its greatest, it stretched from Mesopotamia in the west to the Indus valley in the east. Its capital was at Ctesiphon.

**secular** nonreligious

**shah** ruler, from the Persian word meaning "king"

**Shia Muslims** those who believe that leadership of the Islamic community passed directly to Ali, as the closest blood relative of the Prophet Muhammad, and then through Ali's descendants

**stucco** type of high-quality plaster

**sultan** name given to an Islamic ruler, particularly in the Ottoman Empire

**sumptuous** very luxurious

**Sunni Muslims** those who believe in the successorship of the first four *Khalifahs*

**symmetrical** describes something that has symmetry (balance and proportion in its parts)

**textile** woven or knit cloth

# Index